EMP PROMISES

The Truth About You, Your Desires, and the Lies You've Believed

PARTICIPANT'S GUIDE

PETE WILSON

THOMAS NELSON
Since 1798

NASHVILLE   DALLAS   MEXICO CITY   RIO DE JANEIRO

Published in Nashville, Tennessee, by Thomas Nelson. Thomas Nelson is a registered trademark of Thomas Nelson, Inc.

The publisher is grateful to ECHO Creative Media (Dawn Sherill and Brenda Noel) for writing assistance and collaboration in developing the content for this guide.

Thomas Nelson, Inc. titles may be purchased in bulk for educational, business, fund-raising, or sales promotional use. For information, please e-mail SpecialMarkets@ThomasNelson.com.

Empty Promises Participant's Guide

ISBN: 978-1-4185-5056-1

Printed in the United States of America

12 13 14 15 QG 6 5 4 3 2 1

CONTENTS

INTRODUCTION

Life is a journey. It's a journey that began the moment you were conceived and it will continue throughout your existence. There are certain things your soul longs for on this journey and, whether you've realized it or not, your life is shaped by your search for them—worth, significance, acceptance, love, peace, and beauty are needs felt by all.

Most people have a burning desire to discover a reason for their existence. We feel an all-consuming need at our very core to discover meaning and purpose in life. We search diligently for a source that will meet that need and provide us with the contentment found in knowing who we are and why we're here. Our search may take us down many roads. We may set our sights on people, places, things, situations—any number of things we believe will provide us with the answers to our deepest questions. Wherever our life choices take us, we all continually seek to have our deepest needs met.

I believe that the need to know our purpose and the persistent yearning to have our soul's genuine needs met was placed within us by our Creator God. He wants us to seek for the only thing that will ever truly satisfy our souls—the Person of Jesus Christ.

I'm convinced that only through Him will we ultimately discover our soul's contentment. Our longing souls won't discover rest until we rest in Him.

We are a people wired to worship. All of us treasure something or someone above anything else in our lives. We give our devotion to *somebody* or *something*. So for me, the question isn't, *do we worship?*, the question is, *what are we worshipping?*

Each person in this small group knows the inner hunger to find real answers to the very genuine questions we all share. As we walk together through these few weeks, we will begin to discover truths about our world and about ourselves. We can support and encourage each other along the way as we travel together on this journey toward understanding our search for identity and meaning.

THE EMPTY PROMISES
GROUP EXPERIENCE

Our search for meaning in life can be a lonely quest. We make wrong turns and often end up lost. By joining together with your small group as you pursue the truth behind your desire to find meaning and significance, you join with fellow travelers who are trying to navigate the same road. The support and encouragement you can be for one another cannot be overrated.

While walking this road together, we will encounter real-life situations and emotions that will challenge us to be real with ourselves, each other, and God. I hope you find the time you spend exploring and sharing your hopes, dreams, insights, successes, and failures with your small group to be enlightening and life changing.

In order to create an environment where each person is free to be authentic and open, it's important to agree on some small group ground rules from the start. First, create a "safe zone" for your group. This means that nothing said in the group can be repeated outside the group. Each person's story is his or her own and should only be told by that person. Treating one another with respect and compassion will create a true sense of community that will grow from week to week. In this environment of respect, you should value and protect the emotional, spiritual, and physical space of everyone in the group; no one should devalue a fellow group member in any way, and no one can be touched by another person without permission.

The purpose of your small group is to invite open and honest sharing from your life, but there are some circumstances that call for limited sharing. Steer clear of sharing anything that will put another person in jeopardy, could lead to legal problems, could reflect poorly on someone else, or that you don't have clearance or prior permission to speak about.

Everyone should feel free to share without receiving criticism, advice, or condemnation. You will be on a journey of discovery, telling your own stories and encouraging others to do the same. When someone shares, be sure to thank them for sharing or ask a follow-up question to clarify something they said. Sharing is not an invitation for lecture, correction, or judgment. Your group should be a safe place for all, a place where each person is encouraged to participate as they are able. Avoid letting one person dominate the conversation. Instead, operate according to 1 Corinthians 13:4–7: giving to each other true love, kindness, and patience; bearing, believing, hoping, and enduring all things.

So as we agree to be real with ourselves, each other, and God, let's begin. Let's help one another come to the place where we can all learn to say no to empty promises and yes to God's purpose for our lives.

Leader's Guide available for free download at www.emptypromisesresources.com

HOW TO USE THIS GUIDE

During your small group time, you will watch a DVD together that will introduce the main idea and discussion topic for each session. In this guide, you will find that main idea and discussion topic as well as the discussion questions. Your group may not always get through all of the questions in each session. That is just fine. There may be certain questions that hit home with your particular group and will take up the majority of time for that session. The point is not to get through all the questions. Just use these questions as a way to dig deep into each life within your group. It might help to use your own journal in conjunction with this guide to record any extra notes or thoughts you may have.

At the end of each session, this guide includes five days of personal devotions. These devotions are not meant to be homework. They are simply designed to help you continue thinking, meditating, and reflecting throughout the week about what you're experiencing and learning in your small group. Use these devotions to help you learn more about yourself and God's plan for your life.

Session 1

THE WAITING ROOMS OF LIFE

GETTING STARTED

Watch DVD session 1.

AFTER THE VIDEO

Is there anyone who has not felt the nagging emptiness inside that longs for something: to be a little more beautiful, a little more wealthy, a little more successful, a little more powerful? We always want "a little more." But it is never enough. We look toward tomorrow with hungry eyes, waiting for the thing that will finally satisfy us.

We wait and we wait; and we don't like waiting. Then we get fed up with the wait. Frustration takes over, and we may start feeling our wait is hopeless. If we can't get what we want when we want it, we sometimes take things into our own hands instead of waiting on God's direction. Or we find something else to want. For all our wanting, we remain empty.

11

Consider the Israelites. They were totally ruled by this same inner hunger—the emptiness within that demands to be filled. Israel had actually seen and experienced God's presence. Through Moses, God had led the Israelites from captivity to freedom. They had seen God work. But the minute Moses was out of their sight, the Israelites were forced to wait. When the waiting continued, they decided to find fulfillment in a god of their own making—an idol.

Idolatry is when I look to something that does not have God's power to give me what only God has the power and authority to give.

The Israelites' desire and reaction is really no different from our own. We all seek something to worship; we all seek fulfillment. We seek a feeling of worth and significance. We need to feel we are valued and secure.

God knew about this need. He knew there was an emptiness within all people. He also knew only He could fill the void. He knew there was an ache that haunts every one of us. He knew this longing for purpose, beauty, significance, and peace pulsates through our veins and we would stop at nothing (including building our own golden calves) to fulfill those longings, not even for a moment. So God gave a command: you shall have no other gods before me.

It makes perfect sense that this was God's first command to a newly freed people. We cannot follow His other commands if we break this first one.

Just think about it: your response to God's first eight-word command influences every facet of your life. Idolatry isn't simply a sin. It's what is fundamentally wrong with the human heart.

QUESTIONS FOR DISCUSSION

1. Share about a time in your life when you felt truly satisfied and content.

2. Read Exodus 32:1–6.

   • Have someone in the group recall the events of the exodus from Egypt that had taken place not long before this account.

   • What are some reasons you think the Israelites wanted Aaron to make them gods to worship (v. 1)?

   • Aaron was Moses' brother and helped Moses in leading the people. Why do you think he was willing to do what the people asked of him (vv. 2–5)?

3. Has there ever been a time in your life when you got tired of waiting on God and took matters into your own hands? What happened?

4. Often our search for fulfillment begins with the words "if only I" (for example, "If only I had that . . . I would feel this"). In your search for significance, value, satisfaction, and security, what are your "if only" statements?

5. No one likes to wait. Share a time when waiting was difficult for you. Why was it difficult? Why is waiting such a challenge for us?

6. Why do you think the Israelites chose to worship an idol? In what ways do we follow that same pattern of behavior?

7. How can breaking the first of the Ten Commandments— "You shall have no other gods before me"—keep us from following the other nine?

8. Share about a time when you trusted in an idol (another person, a job, your talent, a hobby, etc.) for something only God could give you. What was the result?

9. What attitude lies at the heart of idolatry? In what ways does this attitude reveal itself in your own life?

10. In what ways do you see idolatry influencing the world around you?

11. How can you begin to identify and break the pattern of idolatry in your own life?

PRAYER

Lord, thank you for creating us with the desire for fulfillment that only you can meet. Please help us through this time together as we recognize the pattern of idolatry in our lives. Show us how to break the pattern and seek only you to fill the emptiness inside. When we get tired of waiting, please help us realize that even waiting times can be a gift bringing growth and closer relationship with you. Help us as we declare our independence from idols through our total dependence on you. Please go with us through this week as we seek you and pray for ourselves and others. Amen.

DAY BY DAY

In our first session, we confronted the reality that we simply hate to wait, and that often leads us to idolatry. Although difficult and frustrating, waiting is worth it when we're living according to God's timetable. The good news is, we are not left on our own. God is with us in the waiting and has even given us great examples of real-life "waiters" in His Word. One such "waiter" is Joshua. His life draws a beautiful picture of the truth in Isaiah 40:31: "But those who hope in the LORD will renew their strength. They will soar on wings like eagles; they will run and not grow weary, they will walk and not be faint." Let's take a walk this week through Joshua's life and see how being a faithful "waiter" helped him avoid idolatry and ultimately helped him soar along the journey God had planned for him.

DAY 1

Exodus 1:8, 9, 11: *Now there arose a new king over Egypt, who did not know Joseph. And he said to his people, "Look, the people of the children of Israel are more and mightier than we. . . . Therefore they set taskmasters over them to afflict them with their burdens. And they built for Pharaoh supply cities, Pithom and Raamses.*

Exodus 14:21, 22: *Then Moses stretched out his hand over the sea; and the Lord caused the sea to go back by a strong east wind all that night, and made the sea into dry land, and the waters were divided. So the children of Israel went into the midst of the sea on the dry ground, and the waters were a wall to them on their right hand and on their left.*

Exodus 17:1a: *Then all the congregation of the children of Israel set out on their journey from the Wilderness of Sin, according to the commandment of the Lord, and camped in Rephidim.*

Exodus 17:8–10: *Now Amalek came and fought with Israel in Rephidim. And Moses said to Joshua, "Choose us some men and go out, fight with Amalek. Tomorrow I will stand on the top of the hill with the rod of God in my hand." So Joshua did as Moses said to him, and fought with Amalek. And Moses, Aaron, and Hur went up to the top of the hill.*

Joshua was one of the Israelites living in captivity in Egypt. He had lived his whole life waiting for God to show up and deliver His people; all the Israelites had waited for generations for their promised Deliverer to appear. As Egyptian slaves, many of the Israelites may have believed the time for hope had passed and no deliverance was on its way. Imagine having to wait a year for someone to keep a promise to you. If waiting just a year for a fulfilled promise could be frustrating, imagine families waiting for generations! It's not so hard to understand why some may have been tempted to give up hope.

Apparently, Joshua was not one of the hopeless ones. We first meet him when the Israelites were attacked by another group of people shortly after God had used Moses to lead the Israelites out of Egypt. Joshua was the first person Moses turned to in planning an attack against their enemy. Joshua must have shown strong character, a godly spirit, and leadership potential for Moses to trust him to lead Israel's fighting men. These character traits were formed in Joshua during a time of captivity and hardship as a slave in Egypt. Instead of switching his allegiance to an Egyptian god or becoming a grumbler in the desert, Joshua apparently used his waiting time to let God continue to form him into the man of character and strength he would ultimately become.

Waiting can be hard for all of us. But like Joshua, we can make the most of our waiting time and let God work in us to form us into the people He created us to be.

QUESTIONS FOR REFLECTION

✳ Think of a situation in which you've had to wait a long time for a promise to be fulfilled. Were you able to maintain hope? Why or why not? How does Joshua's waiting experience in Egypt shed light on your wait?

✳ Why do you think it's so easy to lose faith during a waiting time? What idols are you tempted to build or worship when you are in a waiting time?

✳ Reflect on a challenging experience that God may have used to make you a stronger or more faithful person. How were you able to withstand the challenge? Were you aware at the time that you were growing in character? How can that experience inform your reaction to future challenges or times of waiting?

✳ Are you in a waiting time right now? If so, how can you avoid turning to idolatry to fill the emptiness? In what ways may God be using this time to form or shape you?

✳ If you're not in a waiting time right now, you probably will be at some point. What can you do now to prepare yourself to remain faithful when that time comes?

☀ DAY 2

Exodus 24:12, 13: *Then the Lord said to Moses, "Come up to Me on the mountain and be there; and I will give you tablets of stone, and the law and commandments which I have written, that you may teach them." So Moses arose with his assistant Joshua, and Moses went up to the mountain of God.*

Exodus 32:15–18: *And Moses turned and went down from the mountain, and the two tablets of the Testimony were in his hand. The tablets were written on both sides; on the one side and on the other they were written. Now the tablets were the work of God, and the writing was the writing of God engraved on the tablets. And when Joshua heard the noise of the people as they shouted, he said to Moses, "There is a noise of war in the camp."*

In Exodus 24, we see Joshua accompanying Moses up Mount Sinai. Moses was going there to meet with God, and Joshua was his right hand man on the journey. Joshua waited alone while Moses entered the presence of God. For forty days and forty nights, Moses met with God on the mountain, the Israelites were waiting down below, and Joshua sat by himself in between.

Talk about waiting on the Lord! Forty days and nights is a long time to sit by yourself on a mountainside. Joshua could have let fear or frustration cause him to give up, go back down the mountain, and maybe even join the people in their eventual idolatry. Loneliness could have caused him to give up on

Moses and God. But instead, we once again find him ready and waiting when Moses comes looking for him.

At some point in your life, you will probably face an in-between time when you're not sure exactly what is going on and you're left waiting all by yourself. That is a dangerous time when idolatry can creep into your life. But idolatry is not inevitable. Like Joshua, you can maintain your focus on God and be found ready and waiting when it's time to finally take your next steps.

QUESTIONS FOR REFLECTION

✳ What are some examples of in-between times you've experienced? (Maybe God called you to make a leap of faith and you felt like you were about to go somewhere, do something, or get something, but it just wasn't happening yet.)

✳ During these in-between times, what idols were your biggest temptations? Why?

✳ How do you think Joshua was able to keep himself focused during those forty days and nights? How can that insight help you when you face in-between times of waiting?

☀ DAY 3

Numbers 14:6–10a: *But Joshua the son of Nun and Caleb the son of Jephunneh, who were among those who had spied out the land, tore their clothes; and they spoke to all the congregation of the children of Israel, saying: "The land we passed through to spy out is an exceedingly good land. If the Lord delights in us, then He will bring us into this land and give it to us, 'a land which flows with milk and honey.' Only do not rebel against the Lord, nor fear the people of the land, for they are our bread; their protection has departed from them, and the Lord is with us. Do not fear them." And all the congregation said to stone them with stones.*

Numbers 14:30: *Except for Caleb the son of Jephunneh and Joshua the son of Nun, you shall by no means enter the land which I swore I would make you dwell in.*

Numbers 14:34: *According to the number of the days in which you spied out the land, forty days, for each day you shall bear your guilt one year, namely forty years, and you shall know My rejection.*

Numbers 14:38: *But Joshua the son of Nun and Caleb the son of Jephunneh remained alive, of the men who went to spy out the land.*

Joshua got his first look at the promised land as one of the twelve spies sent on a reconnaissance mission by Moses. He and Caleb were ready and willing to go take the land! But because of the fear and unfaithfulness of others, it would be another forty years before Joshua saw the promised land again.

Joshua did all the right things, but he still had to wait. Through no fault of his own, Joshua spent almost half a century wandering the desert, just waiting to finally go back to that land he fell in love with—the land God had promised to Israel. This provided yet another opportunity for idolatry to take hold in Joshua's life. Forty years is a long time to pursue a promise delayed because of other people. He could have let bitterness build in his heart, or he could have tried to set out on his own to go into the land. But he didn't. Instead, he was able to maintain his focus on God so that he would eventually find his promise fulfilled.

QUESTIONS FOR REFLECTION

✳ Consider a time you had to suffer the consequences of another person's actions. How did knowing you were in that situation through no fault of your own make it easier or more difficult?

✳ What kinds of idols are particularly tempting when you are in one of these "no-fault" times of waiting? What steps can you take to avoid turning to those idols?

✳ What can you learn from Joshua's experience of waiting in the desert? How does his example encourage you?

☀ DAY **4**

Deuteronomy 1:38: *Joshua the son of Nun, who stands before you, he shall go in there. Encourage him, for he shall cause Israel to inherit it.*

Deuteronomy 31: 7, 8: *Then Moses called Joshua and said to him in the sight of all Israel, "Be strong and of good courage, for you must go with this people to the land which the Lord has sworn to their fathers to give them, and you shall cause them to inherit it. And the Lord, He is the One who goes before you. He will be with you, He will not leave you nor forsake you; do not fear nor be dismayed."*

Deuteronomy 34:9: *Now Joshua the son of Nun was full of the spirit of wisdom, for Moses had laid his hands on him; so the children of Israel heeded him, and did as the Lord had commanded Moses.*

It was no secret that Joshua would one day replace Moses as leader of the Israelites. As a matter of fact, God even told Moses that Joshua would be the one to lead the people into the promised land. Joshua knew he had a big future coming, but he didn't take over immediately. He had to wait.

Joshua could have chosen to worship at the altar of his own potential, becoming infatuated with his own abilities. He could have become prideful in his position of power as Moses' protégé. He could have tried to lobby the people to follow him in a coup against Moses. Joshua could have tried to shorten his waiting time by turning to idolatry. But he was able to withstand the temptations and eventually walk into his future in God's time.

Even though we may not see our future mapped out like Joshua did, we are often tempted to try to speed things up or take our next steps before God lays them out for us. But in our waiting times, we can grow in godly wisdom and learn from every experience we have. If we remain focused on God, we can avoid the pitfalls of idolatry and ultimately reach the future He has planned for us.

QUESTIONS FOR REFLECTION

* How do you think Joshua was able to keep himself faithful to function on God's timetable?

* In what situations have you tried to speed up your future? What was the result?

✳ How can the way Joshua handled his "future-in-waiting" encourage you when you're tempted to try to bypass your waiting time?

☼ DAY 5

Joshua 1:1–3: *After the death of Moses the servant of the Lord, it came to pass that the Lord spoke to Joshua the son of Nun, Moses' assistant, saying: "Moses My servant is dead. Now therefore, arise, go over this Jordan, you and all this people, to the land which I am giving to them—the children of Israel. Every place that the sole of your foot will tread upon I have given you, as I said to Moses."*

It was finally time for Joshua to take over as God's leader for the Israelites. He had made the most of his time in waiting and training, and now he was ready to lead the people into the promised land. But his waiting wasn't over. Joshua had to lead the people through more challenges; conquering enemies and taking the land was a long process that took courage and trust in God, even when things didn't make sense.

Read Joshua 6. The battle for Jericho gives us a great picture of this trusting process. Joshua probably didn't understand exactly why they had to wait seven days, but He trusted God and saw the walls of the city fall with just a shout from the Israelite people. Through all his waiting times, Joshua developed the patience and skill needed to lead the people and to trust God even when the battle plan was puzzling. Having been repeatedly encouraged by God to have courage and be strong, Joshua was able to do both, as he successfully kept his focus on God and avoided falling for the empty promises of idols. It is not surprising that in his last speech to the people, he gave them this choice: "Choose for yourselves this day whom you will serve, whether the gods which your fathers served that were on the other side of the River, or the gods of the Amorites, in whose land you dwell. But as for me and my house, we will serve the LORD" (Joshua 24:15).

QUESTIONS FOR REFLECTION

* How do you think all of Joshua's waiting times helped him become a good leader? In what ways have your waiting times made you a stronger person or more mature follower of Christ?

* Have you chosen which God you will serve today? In what ways can you actually serve God, starting right now?

THE GOOD LIFE

G R O U P   D I S C U S S I O N

GETTING STARTED

Watch DVD session 2.

AFTER THE VIDEO

I want the good life. Status. Respect. Love. Appreciation. Attention. Admiration. I want all these guys to want to be me. I want the good life. And I know how to make it happen. First, they need to know I'm here. I need to be seen. Sure, I may not be at the front of the line . . . yet. But soon it will be my turn. I'm proving my worth—anyone should be able to see it.

Okay, this is better. I'm closer to the front of the line now. Everyone back there envies me. Just a few more feet and I'll have everything I need. And when I leave this line, I'm taking it all with me. Then everyone will know I've got the good life. It's mine! All mine!

> The bottom line is that every single human being has an unbelievable capacity for self-deception.

Wait a minute—what's he got? I don't have that! You mean I need more? There's another line? I have to do all this again? Where does it all end? How does an ant finally get the good life?

This is not just the story of an ant. This is a picture of reality for countless people today, even many Christians. Our media presents us with a picture of the good life, and we immediately line up. We pursue a life we think is desirable: better career, bigger house, nicer car, perfect body, cult-like following, and limitless funds to keep it all going. But in the end, we still struggle with a gnawing sense of emptiness.

To satisfy this emptiness, we are tempted to turn to more empty promises to hide our pain. In order to find some type of worth or value, we turn to others to gain that elusive approval we think will fill and comfort us. There are few things we fear as much as we fear being unwanted, rejected, and alone.

QUESTIONS FOR DISCUSSION

1. Have you ever been willing to stand in a ridiculously long line for something that was probably not worth it? Maybe it was the latest hot Christmas gift or the newest electronic gadget. Why were you willing to stand in that line?

2. In what areas of life have you expected to find fulfillment only to be left disappointed and disillusioned? Career? Marriage? Parenthood? Wealth? Popularity? Share a bit of your story.

3. In your current life situation, how would you define "the good life"? How would you have defined it five years ago? How might it look five years from now?

4. In what ways has the media influenced your perception of the good life?

5. How can our pursuit of what we perceive as the good life result in idolatry?

6. How can you identify some of these hidden idols in your life?

7. Honestly share with the group:

- What occupies your mind? What do you spend time daydreaming about?

- Who do you tend to be jealous of?

- How do you spend most of your time?

- Where does the majority of your money go?

How do you feel about your answers to these questions?

8. Why do you think loneliness and rejection inspire such fear in everyone?

9. What (or Who) can conquer that fear?

PRAYER

Father, so much in this life leaves us empty and cold. Thank you for providing what truly fulfills and brings us satisfaction—the warmth of your presence. Help us to be willing to identify our hidden idols and deny them as we find our true acceptance and value in you. Please help us to define the good life based on your promises, your life, and your love—which will never leave us empty. Thank you for giving us courage and wisdom to be real with you, ourselves, and each other as we go throughout this week and the rest of this study. Amen.

DAY BY DAY

The search for fulfillment is nothing new. People have always looked for meaning and purpose in life. We see this search played out clearly in the life of Solomon. He was David's son and God's appointed king of Israel. He had been granted extraordinary wisdom by God, yet he foolishly seized opportunities to try every empty promise from every idol available. Let's follow Solomon's journey to see where he ultimately realized meaning and purpose could be found.

☼ DAY 1

Ecclesiastes 1:12, 13a: *I, the Preacher, was king over Israel in Jerusalem. And I set my heart to seek and search out by wisdom concerning all that is done under heaven.*

Ecclesiastes 1:16–18: *I communed with my heart, saying, "Look, I have attained greatness, and have gained more wisdom than all who were before me in Jerusalem. My heart has understood great wisdom and knowledge." And I set my heart to know wisdom and to know madness and folly. I perceived that this also is grasping for the wind. For in much wisdom is much grief, And he who increases knowledge increases sorrow.*

Earlier in his life, Solomon had the opportunity to ask God for anything, and he asked for wisdom. So God made Solomon extremely wise. While that was certainly an amazing blessing that served Solomon well, it could not fill his need for meaning and purpose.

As the verses above show, Solomon set out on a journey of learning, expecting that wisdom could teach him and give him everything. But the more he learned, the more he realized that acquiring additional wisdom was not his ultimate purpose; wisdom could never fulfill him. Rather than finding fulfillment for the empty parts of his soul, he found more and more grief. Wisdom for wisdom's sake will never satisfy.

Have you ever tried to grab hold of the wind? If your neighbors saw you attempting this, they might think you had gone off the deep end. The wind blows by you, but you can't catch it in your hand. You can't grasp it. Trying to grasp the wind would be an exercise in futility. That's how Solomon eventually saw the search for wisdom alone—as an exercise in futility that can never completely bring us true meaning or purpose.

Pursuing godly wisdom as we seek to follow Jesus is not a bad thing. Jesus Himself, when He lived on earth, "increased in wisdom and stature, and in favor with God and men" (Luke 2:52). But if our desire for wisdom becomes the focus of our lives, then it loses its true value and can become a breeding ground for idolatry. Rather than elevating wisdom to the level of a god in our lives, we can pursue godly wisdom as part of our overall desire to follow and serve the one true God.

QUESTIONS FOR REFLECTION

✳ Why do you believe Solomon chose to ask God for wisdom? What do you think you would have asked for? Why?

✳ What is the difference between seeking godly wisdom and seeking wisdom for wisdom's sake?

✳ Which ofthese two types of wisdom have you spent more time seeking?

✳ What role does wisdom play in your life right now? How can you make godly wisdom a part of your journey of faith rather than a destination?

☀ DAY 2

1 Kings 11:1–6: *But King Solomon loved many foreign women, as well as the daughter of Pharaoh: women of the Moabites, Ammonites, Edomites, Sidonians, and Hittites—from the nations of whom the Lord had said to the children of Israel, "You shall not intermarry with them, nor they with you. Surely they will turn away your hearts after their gods." Solomon clung to these in love. And he had seven hundred wives, princesses, and three hundred concubines; and his wives turned away his heart. For it was so, when Solomon was old, that his wives turned his heart after other gods; and his heart was not loyal to the Lord his God, as was the heart of his father David. For Solomon went after Ashtoreth the goddess of the Sidonians, and after Milcom the abomination of the Ammonites. Solomon did evil in the sight of the Lord, and did not fully follow the Lord, as did his father David.*

1 Kings 11:9, 10: *So the Lord became angry with Solomon, because his heart had turned from the Lord God of Israel, who had appeared to him twice, and had commanded him concerning* *this thing, that he should not go after other gods; but he did not keep what the Lord had commanded.*

As we learned in Day 1's personal devotion, all of Solomon's wisdom was not enough to bring him meaning and purpose. Today we see that his great wisdom wasn't even enough to keep him from directly disobeying a clear and serious command from God: not to marry foreign women who would influence him to serve idols.

These women turned Solomon's head and then they turned his heart away from God. But Solomon was absolutely responsible for his own actions. It was his decision to have "seven hundred wives, princesses, and three hundred concubines" (1 Kings 11:3). It would have been bad enough to disobey God's command by marrying one foreign woman who served an idol—disobedience is disobedience—but Solomon didn't stop there. If one woman could have turned his heart from God, how much more so a thousand women!

Solomon didn't just flirt with trying to find satisfaction in lust and romantic love. He went all out. He allowed his infatuation with women to lead to a fascination with their worthless idols. He allowed lust to become an idol in his life, which led to even more idolatry.

We may not be in Solomon's position of having hundreds of concubines and spouses, but do not be misled: lust and romantic love can quickly become idols in our lives. When we allow our fascination with someone of the opposite sex to become our entire focus, we are really looking for meaning and purpose in another place that will only leave us empty in the end. When we think that one more sexual encounter will be the one that finally satisfies us, we are in the midst of that vicious cycle of emptiness that will never end. Until we realize our true meaning and purpose only comes through Jesus Christ, we will remain empty and wanting. The idols of lust and romantic love were crafty enough to trip up the wisest man in the world. We would be wise to guard ourselves.

QUESTIONS FOR REFLECTION

* Why do you think Solomon's wisdom didn't help him avoid idolatry? How do you think Solomon may have rationalized his actions?

* How did Solomon's idol of lust lead to even more idolatry?

* How have the idols of lust or romantic love tried to take over your life? What rationalizations have you used to attempt to justify your worship of these idols?

✴ How have these idols left you feeling empty? How can you prepare yourself to continually turn away from these idols as you follow Christ?

 DAY **3**

Ecclesiastes 2:1–3: *I said in my heart, "Come now, I will test you with mirth; therefore enjoy pleasure"; but surely, this also was vanity. I said of laughter—"Madness!"; and of mirth, "What does it accomplish?" I searched in my heart how to gratify my flesh with wine, while guiding my heart with wisdom, and how to lay hold on folly, till I might see what was good for the sons of men to do under heaven all the days of their lives.*

In today's reading we find Solomon continuing on his journey for meaning and purpose. Wisdom alone didn't work. Lust and romantic love didn't work. Now we find him seeking pleasure in general. He was ready to try anything and everything. He even says, "Whatever my eyes desired I did not keep from them. I did not withhold my heart from any pleasure" (Ecclesiastes 2:10a).

He tried drinking and throwing himself into the party scene of his day. But all the alcohol and all the superficial laughter and all the worldly pleasures still left him empty. He found this part of his search just more "vanity," or meaninglessness.

If we're honest, most of us would have to admit being at least temporarily fooled or fascinated by the idol of pleasure. We see examples of this around us every day. To fill the emptiness inside, we may turn to alcohol, drugs, sex, or just one party after another. But every party ends, and the emptiness remains. True pleasure, not just physical or emotional feel-good moments, comes with true peace and contentment. And true peace and contentment come only in relationship with the one true God.

QUESTIONS FOR REFLECTION

* When have you sought to fill the emptiness in your life with earthly pleasures (such as drinking, drugs, sex, partying, food, shopping)? What was the result?

* What emotions did you have during this time?

* What is it about pleasure that can trick us into believing it can bring us fulfillment?

✳ What is the difference between temporary pleasure and true peace and contentment from God? What steps can you take away from worldly pleasures and toward true contentment?

DAY 4

Ecclesiastes 2:4–9: *I made my works great, I built myself houses, and planted myself vineyards. I made myself gardens and orchards, and I planted all kinds of fruit trees in them. I made myself water pools from which to water the growing trees of the grove. I acquired male and female servants, and had servants born in my house. Yes, I had greater possessions of herds and flocks than all who were in Jerusalem before me. I also gathered for myself silver and gold and the special treasures of kings and of the provinces. I acquired male and female singers, the delights of the sons of men, and musical instruments of all kinds. So I became great and excelled more than all who were before me in Jerusalem. Also my wisdom remained with me.*

Ecclesiastes 2:11: *Then I looked on all the works that my hands had done and on the labor in which I had toiled; and indeed all was vanity and grasping for the wind. There was no profit under the sun.*

Again in today's readings we see Solomon engaged in the search for meaning. He has kept his wisdom, but once again it cannot keep him from worshipping at the altar of another meaningless idol: riches.

Being the king was not a bad gig. Solomon built a huge and prosperous kingdom. He was the poster boy for that day's Lifestyles of the Rich and Famous. Anything he wanted to build or buy, he built or bought. He had servants galore so he would not have to lift a finger unless he wanted to. It was not easy to accumulate all this great wealth, but once he did, you might think Solomon would finally be satisfied. But it was not so.

Solomon could walk out onto his rooftop and survey his kingdom. He could look over all his buildings and orchards and command all his servants to bring him anything he wanted. But still, something was missing. For all he had, Solomon still felt himself trying to grasp the elusive wind. It was just not possible to find meaning in all his wealth and power. All his profits were of no profit to him in the end.

QUESTIONS FOR REFLECTION

✳ Solomon was quite the celebrity in his time. How do you think Solomon was perceived by the average people in his kingdom? Reading Ecclesiastes, do you think that supposed perception was valid? What types of similar and possibly faulty perceptions do you have about celebrities in our culture? Why are those your perceptions, and what might be faulty about them?

* In what ways have you tried to find meaning or purpose in working to achieve wealth or status? How can knowing Solomon's experience help you avoid the empty promises of wealth and accumulation?

* Why can't riches ultimately fill the emptiness in your life? What can fill that emptiness?

☼ DAY **5**

Ecclesiastes 12:13: *Let us hear the conclusion of the whole matter: fear God and keep His commandments, for this is man's all.*

This week we have followed Solomon on a search for meaning. We have seen him repeatedly grasp at the wind by falling for the empty promises of wisdom for wisdom's sake, lust and romantic love, worldly pleasures, wealth, and status. All of these things can look great from the outside. They tempt us with the possibility of final fulfillment and true peace. But they are all false. They can back up none of their promises. Solomon was just as empty after trying them as he was before.

But there was finally a light at the end of the tunnel. Solomon did find the final answer. He tells us in his own words "the conclusion of the whole matter." Where does meaning live? Where can we find purpose? What can we do to get rid of our emptiness? Go to God. Or go back to God. He created everything that is and He created you. He knows everything about everything, and He knows exactly what you need and exactly what your purpose is. Rather than chasing after idols and their empty promises, you can finally rest in the knowledge that true peace, contentment, meaning, and purpose are waiting for you—waiting right in the hand of God, where He longs to hold you as well.

QUESTIONS FOR REFLECTION

✳ Which of Solomon's searches hit closest to home with you? Why?

✳ Do you ever doubt that God would want to take you back after you've chased empty idols? Read Luke 15:11–32. How can Jesus' words encourage you to go back to God?

✳ Say a prayer expressing your heart to God. Confess the idol searches you've gone on and admit that you can only find meaning in Him. Ask Him to help you keep your focus on Him.

RELIGION LIES

GROUP DISCUSSION

GETTING STARTED

Watch DVD session 3.

AFTER THE VIDEO

Life can be a vicious cycle. Like the man in today's video, we walk habitually through our days, checking off our list of duties. When that's all there is to life, it's a sad way to live; it's an even sadder way to approach God. Every time we think we've accomplished everything on our spiritual checklist, we find it has only grown and we are no closer to completing it than when we began.

When our spiritual lives are nothing more than a treadmill of endless effort, our attempt to reach God leaves us running in place—exhausting ourselves but never arriving anywhere. Religion is nothing more than a spiritual treadmill that leaves us weary and wanting. It is our attempt to rely on the rightness of our own acts or doctrines instead of trusting in God Himself. Though it might seem like just a minor mis-step, this is a deadly mistake.

We all have a desperate desire to be loved and accepted. When religion rules us (becomes an idol), we assume God's love is conditional. So we attempt to earn His love and grace. But no matter how hard we struggle, we are engaged in a hopeless pursuit. We do not have to earn God's love; we need to realize He pursues us with His love through Jesus. We can be freed from the treadmill of effort when we recognize Jesus is truly enough. Nothing is missing from God's love toward us. It is completed in His Son. It is not Jesus plus anything that saves us or defines who we are; it is just Jesus. Anything else is an empty promise.

> Religion always complicates what God has made simple. Religion always wants to elevate an action or experience to an idol-like status by adding it to Jesus.

QUESTIONS FOR DISCUSSION

1. Have you ever "wiped out" on a treadmill? Share the story.

2. How do you know if you're stuck on a spiritual treadmill?

Ask yourself:

- Deep down, do you believe you can earn God's love through obedience?

- Do you believe being a good, moral person increases your chances of getting into heaven?

- Do you think your faith in or obedience to God will bring you better health, more wealth, power, and control?

- Do you find yourself regularly battling uncertainty about your standing before God?

3. In what ways do you attempt to earn God's love? How can this be a "deadly mistake"?

4. What has made you believe God's love is conditional? What affect has this had on your spiritual journey?

5. What you do *with* Jesus is more important than what you do *for* Him. How should this truth affect your spiritual journey?

PRAYER

Father God, we thank you for freeing us from the treadmill of effort. We praise you for your free and unconditional love. Increase our desire to serve you, obey you, and love you. Thank you for your Son, through whom we have all we could ever need. Help us walk through this week with the peace that comes from leaving the treadmill behind and stepping out into your full and complete promise. Help us deny the empty promise of religion. Be with us and guide us. In Jesus' name we pray. Amen.

DAY BY DAY

In session 3 we learned that religion lies to us. It tells us that we have to keep up with an unachievable checklist in order to be right with God. The truth is that God pursues us with His grace. We can't earn His grace, we can only accept it. He has been pursuing people with His grace since the beginning. This week we are going to see Jesus embody this truth as He reaches out to the last people we would expect Him to pursue. And hopefully we will experience a fresh appreciation and understanding of His truly amazing grace.

☀ DAY 1

Acts 9:1–9: *Then Saul, still breathing threats and murder against the disciples of the Lord, went to the high priest and asked letters from him to the synagogues of Damascus, so that if he found any who were of the Way, whether men or women, he might bring them bound to Jerusalem. As he journeyed he came near Damascus, and suddenly a light shone around him from heaven. Then he fell to the ground, and heard a voice saying to him, "Saul, Saul, why are you persecuting Me?" And he said, "Who are You, Lord?" Then the Lord said, "I am Jesus, whom you are persecuting. It is hard for you to kick against the goads." So he, trembling and astonished, said, "Lord, what do*

You want me to do?" Then the Lord said to him, "Arise and go into the city, and you will be told what you must do." And the men who journeyed with him stood speechless, hearing a voice but seeing no one. Then Saul arose from the ground, and when his eyes were opened he saw no one. But they led him by the hand and brought him into Damascus. And he was three days without sight, and neither ate nor drank.

Saul was literally making a career out of persecuting Christians. As an up-and-coming Pharisee (Jewish religious leader), he was making his mark by making life dangerous for Christ's followers. At this point, we might expect God to intervene in a way that stopped Saul from persecuting His followers and maybe even exact a bit of divine vengeance. But that is not what happened. Instead of exacting vengeance, Jesus reached out to Saul with grace.

After his conversion, Saul went by the name of Paul, and he became God's missionary to the Gentiles (non-Jewish people). He also became the Holy Spirit–inspired author of much of the New Testament. Paul had been an active and ardent enemy of God right up to the time Jesus reached out to him. As a Pharisee, he was accustomed to being measured by his religious works, but Jesus offered him a whole new measurement scale. Paul would spend the rest of his life marveling at the amazing amount of grace that a holy and loving God continually offers to all people, even His enemies.

Paul did amazing things for God and His kingdom, but he didn't do them to earn his salvation or to get brownie points from God. Rather, he did them in response to God's love and grace. Paul was able to climb off the treadmill of religion and instead run toward the goal of knowing Christ more and more. Religion could never accomplish this transformation. It was all the grace of God.

QUESTIONS FOR REFLECTION

✳ Why do you think God reached out to Saul in grace rather than vengeance?

✳ What can you learn about God's love from Saul/Paul's life?

✳ What's the difference between working in response to religion and working in response to grace? How have you seen that distinction play out in your life?

✴ Consider your own experience with God's grace. Are you continuing to live in the freedom and peace His grace brings? Why or why not? If not, what steps can you take to refresh yourself in God's grace?

DAY 2

> **John 8:10, 11**: *When Jesus had raised Himself up and saw no one but the woman, He said to her, "Woman, where are those accusers of yours? Has no one condemned you?" She said, "No one, Lord." And Jesus said to her, "Neither do I condemn you; go and sin no more."*

In John 8:3–11, the religious leaders of the day wanted to trap Jesus in an awkward situation in which He would do or say something they could use against Him. So they brought to Jesus a woman who had been caught in an adulterous relationship. You may expect that Jesus' reaction would be one of righteous indignation, that He would be shocked at the woman's sin and ready to condemn her to the consequences of her actions.

Instead, peace ruled the day. Not only did Jesus reach out in grace to the woman, He also taught the religious leaders a much-needed lesson. None of them were without sin, so none of them were in a position to look down their noses in judgment of this woman. If anyone had the right to judge her it was Jesus, being God in human form. But instead of judging her based on her sin, He forgave her based on His grace.

He did not approve of her actions or encourage her to continue them. As a matter of fact, He made a point to tell her to keep it together and "sin no more." Grace wasn't a license for her to sin as much as she wanted. Rather, it was the basis of forgiveness and the motivation of right living in the future. Where society saw a sinner to be stoned, Jesus saw a person to be saved.

QUESTIONS FOR REFLECTION

* What do you think the religious leaders expected Jesus to do? Why?

* How do you think the woman felt when all her accusers began to walk away and when Jesus spoke words of forgiveness rather than accusation?

* How have you been overwhelmed by God's forgiveness in your own life?

DAY 3

John 4:7–10: *A woman of Samaria came to draw water. Jesus said to her, "Give Me a drink." For His disciples had gone away into the city to buy food. Then the woman of Samaria said to Him, "How is it that You, being a Jew, ask a drink from me, a Samaritan woman?" For Jews have no dealings with Samaritans. Jesus answered and said to her, "If you knew the gift of God, and who it is who says to you, 'Give Me a drink,' you would have asked Him, and He would have given you living water."*

Read John 4. In that chapter, Jesus and His disciples were traveling through Samaria. This was a big deal, because in that day Jews would typically try to avoid Samaria. Jews and Samaritans were related people groups, but they held a great deal of animosity toward one another. That is why the woman at the well was so surprised that Jesus, being a Jew, would even talk to her. Added to that, Jesus pointed out a little later in the conversation that the lady had been married multiple times and was at that time living with a man who wasn't her husband. The fact that He was still willing to talk to her, even knowing the scandalous details of her life, was also amazing.

Jesus could have treated this woman with disdain or haughty judgment. But that was not His spirit. Instead, He reached out to her with grace. He didn't gloss over her sin or pretend like everything was okay. But He also didn't write her off because of that sin. Rather, He let her know she could find the answer for life only in Him. He is the Messiah. He wanted her to understand that once she put her trust in Him, she wouldn't have to keep trying to fill her heart's emptiness with relationships, men, or anything else. By the grace of God, she would find contentment in Him alone.

Not only did Jesus' grace touch this one Samaritan woman, but through her witness, many of the Samaritans believed in Him, and their lives were never the same.

QUESTIONS FOR REFLECTION

* Can you relate to the Samaritan woman in this story? If so, how?

* Do you ever believe deep down that God won't forgive you because of your deepest, darkest sins? How can the truth in John 4 encourage you to fully embrace God's grace in your life?

* Has your life been a witness to the grace of God? If so, how? If not, how could it be?

DAY **4**

Matthew 9:9–13: *As Jesus passed on from there, He saw a man named Matthew sitting at the tax office. And He said to him, "Follow Me." So he arose and followed Him. Now it happened, as Jesus sat at the table in the house, that behold, many tax collectors and sinners came and sat down with Him and His disciples. And when the Pharisees saw it, they said to His disciples, "Why does your Teacher eat with tax collectors and sinners?" When Jesus heard that, He said to them, "Those who are well have no need of a physician, but those who are sick. But go and learn what this means: 'I desire mercy and not sacrifice.' For I did not come to call the righteous, but sinners, to repentance."*

Tax collectors have never been popular people. Their job is to take money from people, so of course people are not happy to see them coming. Often in Matthew's day, tax collectors were also cheaters. They could charge people extra taxes and pocket the difference. They could sell out their own people to raise themselves up in the ruling government. Many of them were basically schemers. So when Jesus called Matthew to be His disciple, many people probably viewed it as a puzzling choice.

As if having a tax collector for a disciple weren't bold enough, Jesus then proceeded to eat dinner with a whole house full of tax collectors and other assorted sinners. The Pharisees probably could not believe their eyes. Shocked and angered at Jesus' questionable choices for dinner companions, they asked Jesus' disciples why He would associate with such

people. Jesus answered for Himself by telling the religious offi-
cials that these were the very people He came to save.

We are all sinners; none of us are righteous on our own
(Romans 3:10). Just because these particular people were
identified by the rest of society as undesirable didn't mean
their sins were unforgivable; and it certainly didn't make their
sins any worse than those of the Pharisees or anyone else.
Jesus came "to seek and to save that which was lost" (Luke
19:10). "That which was lost" is all of us—all mankind,
including tax collectors, Pharisees, you, and me. The level of
our sin never determines the level of God's grace.

QUESTIONS FOR REFLECTION

✳ Who would be our society's equivalent of the "tax collectors and sinners"? Why are we prone to categorize each
   other according to our sins?

✳ Since Jesus reaches out to even the "unlikeables" of society,
   how should we as Christ-followers interact with everyone?

✳ Is the fact that we cannot earn God's grace or limit its power a freeing thought for you? Why or why not?

 ## DAY 5

Philippians 2:5–8: *Let this mind be in you which was also in Christ Jesus, who, being in the form of God, did not consider it robbery to be equal with God, but made Himself of no reputation, taking the form of a bondservant, and coming in the likeness of men. And being found in appearance as a man, He humbled Himself and became obedient to the point of death, even the death of the cross.*

Luke 23:34a: *Then Jesus said, "Father, forgive them, for they do not know what they do."*

Jesus didn't extend His grace to us without cost to Himself. He left the perfection of heaven to come to earth. That was a huge sacrifice. He took His sacrifice even further when He came to earth as a man, and a servant at that. But He didn't stop there. He lived a perfect life, defeating every temptation. Then He sacrificed Himself for our sins in the most painful and humiliating way—crucifixion. In the midst of this sacrifice, He prayed for forgiveness for the very people crucifying Him, knowing that the sacrifice He was making is what enabled that prayer to be answered.

He did all of this because He loves us and He wants to extend His grace to us, to free us from sin and give us eternal life with Him. Jesus did all that. There's not one thing we can do to match it, limit it, or add to it. We just have to choose whether to accept it or reject it.

Religion may hand you a three-mile-long checklist of acts to perform to make you begin to feel worthy of God's salvation. But there is only one box to check off on grace's checklist: trust Him. Everything else we do is in response to this great love the Father has for us. We don't act to earn His love; we act in response to His love.

QUESTIONS FOR REFLECTION

✳ Have you ever thought about everything Jesus gave up to save us? How does that knowledge affect how you relate to Him and His grace?

✳ Why does it seem natural for us to feel like we need to do something to earn grace? How is that a false belief?

✳ How does the difference between grace and religion play out in your life?

✳ What steps can you take to live according to grace rather than religion?

MONEY

GROUP DISCUSSION

GETTING STARTED

Watch DVD session 4.

AFTER THE VIDEO

The love of money can often creep into our hearts until it becomes the ultimate focus of life. Whether we live in severe poverty or abundant wealth, money can become a ruling force and the most tyrannical idol we choose to serve. One of Jesus' most popular teaching topics was money.

> The idolatry of money is not only the love of money but the excessive anxiety over it.

None of us are safe from the temptation of trying to find peace and security by placing our trust in the power of money instead of the power of God. If money could buy peace, the wealthiest among us would enjoy continual, never-ending peace. Look around you. Is that the case?

Because we have bought into the lie that more money equals more peace, we are on a continual quest for a bit more money. But when our supply increases, we still need just a bit more. Whether blue-collar worker, jet-set tycoon, or victim of utter poverty, the quest is often the same: just a little bit more.

The problem is we end up seeking money instead of peace. There is *zero* correlation between money and true peace. Even while eating dirt cookies in a ragged tent, the Indian family in the video knew true peace. They possessed more than money could possibly buy. They knew peace is not found in dollar signs but in the sign of the cross.

QUESTIONS FOR DISCUSSION

1. Why do you think it is considered bad form to tell others the size of your bank account?

2. Is it possible money has become an idol in your life? Ask yourself:

- Does my fear of not having enough often impede my desire to be generous? How can I overcome this fear?

- Do I have plenty of money in the bank but no peace in my heart? What causes this?

- How much more money would I need to feel secure?

- Do I spend more time thinking about what I don't have than thanking God for what I do have? Why?

What do these answers reveal about your attitude toward money?

3. Where has the quest for peace led you financially and spiritually?

4. Why do you believe it is so easy for us to fall into the money pit—the lie that more money will bring us peace?

5. Read Ecclesiastes 5:10. What insight can you gain from this verse?

6. Share with the group your definition of true peace.

PRAYER

Lord, I thank you for providing what I need. Help me to remember that, no matter how much I have, if I don't have you, I have nothing. Keep me focused on you and your power in my life. Guard my heart and keep me from falling into the trap of trusting in money instead of in your love for me. Fill me with the peace only you can bring. I ask these things in the name of your Son, Jesus. Amen.

DAY BY DAY

Money is a necessity in this life, but it should never be our focus. We will never find the peace and security we desire through the pursuit of wealth, status, or power—the things money offers. We should live our lives in the pursuit of God's eternal kingdom. When we focus on God's kingdom, we will see the things of this world exactly as they are—temporary. A good question to ask yourself when determining the important things in your life is, "In terms of eternity, how much does this really mean?"

☀ DAY 1

1 Timothy 6:10: *For the love of money is a root of all kinds of evil, for which some have strayed from the faith in their greediness, and pierced themselves through with many sorrows.*

Psalm 10:3: *For the wicked boasts of his heart's desire; He blesses the greedy and renounces the Lord.*

Proverbs 1:19: *So are the ways of everyone who is greedy for gain; it takes away the life of its owners.*

"I want what I want when I want it." Most likely, no one would actually say those words, but how many of us live them? Far too often, we are so ruled by what we want that we become consumed with the pursuit of meeting our own desires. When those desires are determined by the world's perception of what is important, we end up spending our lives "grasping for the wind" (Ecclesiastes 6:9). In the end, we find ourselves surrounded by tomorrow's landfill debris and no closer to finding meaning in life or peace for our souls.

This is a sad commentary on humanity. Within each of us is the need to find meaning and purpose; but we try to find our answers in places that have no more to offer than fleeting, empty promises. We focus on worldly treasures and do all we can to gain them only to find ourselves caught up in a vicious cycle: we struggle, we acquire, we find ourselves empty, and the process begins again. We have become a kind of being that is forever hungry and never satisfied—we are consumers.

The scariest part of society's materialistic identity is that it bears a striking resemblance to the description of our enemy: "The devil walks about like a roaring lion, seeking whom he may devour" (1 Peter 5:8). As we attempt to consume the riches the world offers, we are actually taking on the character of the one who wants to consume us. We cooperate with his scheme as we allow our worldly desires to distract us from the only One who can fill our need for meaning and purpose. We grasp at the enemy's empty promises. But our hands remain empty and our hearts unfulfilled.

QUESTIONS FOR REFLECTION

✳ Have you ever known true want in your life? If you were to experience the severe poverty of the Indian family from our video, what do you believe your reaction would be?

✳ In what ways do you find yourself grasping at the empty promise of money?

✳ Consider Paul's words, "The love of money is a root of all kinds of evil." How do you see this truth in action in the world around you?

✳ In what way have you fallen for the enemy's materialistic schemes in your own life? What steps can you take to overcome this?

☼ DAY 2

Isaiah 26:3: *You will keep him in perfect peace, whose mind is stayed on You, because he trusts in You.*

Matthew 6:24: *No one can serve two masters; for either he will hate the one and love the other, or else he will be loyal to the one and despise the other. You cannot serve God and mammon.*

Luke 12:27, 28: *Consider the lilies, how they grow: they neither toil nor spin; and yet I say to you, even Solomon in all his glory was not arrayed like one of these. If then God so clothes the grass, which today is in the field and tomorrow is thrown into the oven, how much more will He clothe you, O you of little faith?*

John 14:27: *Peace I leave with you, My peace I give to you; not as the world gives do I give to you. Let not your heart be troubled, neither let it be afraid.*

Philippians 4:6, 7: *Be anxious for nothing, but in everything by prayer and supplication, with thanksgiving, let your requests be made known to God; and the peace of God, which surpasses all understanding, will guard your hearts and minds through Christ Jesus.*

Wow! Jesus didn't mince words about the effect of allowing the quest for riches to rule our hearts. He said it straight, "You cannot serve God and mammon." If you are enslaved to your quest for riches ("mammon"), you have bound yourself to something other than God. And if you are enslaved, your life is no longer your own.

How sad that we allow anything to come before our relationship with the Lord. You see, it's not just those who are wealthy who give their lives over to the pursuit of "mammon," it's also those who worry continually about how to pay the bills, those who obsess about IRAs and bank account balances, and those who are so afraid of the loss of material things that they will do whatever it takes to hold on to them. Whenever we allow the things of this world to replace our relationship with God and our trust in Him, we have invited them to be our master.

To avoid being a slave to those things that will not last, you must trust God. If you trust Him and believe His Word, you realize He is fully deserving of your trust; He loves you and will always provide whatever you truly need. And what you need most is Him.

QUESTIONS FOR REFLECTION

* How can realizing God's limitless love for you enable you to walk without fear and avoid the trap of idolizing "mammon"?

✳ Most of us are enslaved to "mammon" to some degree. How does this slavery show up in your life?

✳ How can considering the things God has provided in the past help you to walk in faith for today?

✳ Have you ever experienced the peace that surpasses understanding? Do you believe it is possible to know this kind of peace at all times? How?

✳ What lies at the heart of perfect peace?

☀ DAY **3**

Mark 10:17–22: *Now as He was going out on the road, one came running, knelt before Him, and asked Him, "Good Teacher, what shall I do that I may inherit eternal life?" So Jesus said to him, "Why do you call Me good? No one is good but One, that is, God. You know the commandments: 'Do not commit adultery,' 'Do not murder,' 'Do not steal,' 'Do not bear false witness,' 'Do not defraud,' 'Honor your father and your mother.'" And he answered and said to Him, "Teacher, all these things I have kept from my youth." Then Jesus, looking at him, loved him, and said to him, "One thing you lack: Go your way, sell whatever you have and give to the poor, and you will have treasure in heaven; and come, take up the cross, and follow Me." But he was sad at this word, and went away sorrowful, for he had great possessions.*

Reading this story can be a bit confusing. Was Jesus actually telling this man he could buy eternal life? Of course not. Eternal life is found only in Jesus. But Jesus wanted this man to look closely at himself. He wanted him to realize how important all his stuff had become in his life.

You may imagine if Jesus stood in front of you and asked you to sell everything, you'd have a garage sale tomorrow. But is that the case? What about your house? What about your car? What about all those keepsakes gathering dust in the attic? Would you actually sell them without a second thought? As is true of most of us, if you're honest, you couldn't claim you'd follow Jesus' instructions any better than the young man in the story.

Whether we mean to or not, we can become strongly attached to things. Houses and cars come to mean security; keepsakes seem to add meaning and emotional connection to our lives; stylish clothing and jewelry equal status. Without realizing what has happened, we can start depending on things to bring peace and contentment to our lives.

QUESTIONS FOR REFLECTION

* If you lost your job tomorrow, what would be your reaction?

* If your home burned to the ground, what things would you miss the most? Why?

* In what ways have money and the things you own become a source of peace and security? Why is this wrong?

Session 4

✳ How can you guard against falling for the empty promises of money?

 DAY **4**

Matthew 6:19–21: *Do not lay up for yourselves treasures on earth, where moth and rust destroy and where thieves break in and steal; but lay up for yourselves treasures in heaven, where neither moth nor rust destroys and where thieves do not break in and steal. For where your treasure is, there your heart will be also.*

Matthew 6:31–34: *Therefore do not worry, saying, "What shall we eat?" or "What shall we drink?" or "What shall we wear?" For after all these things the Gentiles seek. For your heavenly Father knows that you need all these things. But seek first the kingdom of God and His righteousness, and all these things shall be added to you. Therefore do not worry about tomorrow, for tomorrow will worry about its own things. Sufficient for the day is its own trouble.*

Have you ever noticed how much time you spend thinking about, planning for, and worrying over tomorrow? As you walk through the next couple of days, pay attention to where your thoughts travel. Your thoughts reflect what you value; they will point directly to what you treasure most.

Take a moment to read Proverbs 23:4–7. Consider verse 7: "As he thinks in his heart, so is he." The writer is speaking of one who trusts in things rather than God. In fact, the first few verses of Proverbs 23 talk about people who focus on things that will only leave them empty and wanting. Their thoughts are filled with plans for tomorrow and what they will gain; they may feast on a king's delicacies, but their hearts will remain empty.

When we spend all our mental energy focusing on tomorrow, we lose today and still wind up empty. We need to remember that our relationship with God is in the present: it is only now that we can serve Him, love Him, and grow closer to Him. None of us are promised tomorrow, and yesterday is just a memory. The only life we really have is today.

QUESTIONS FOR REFLECTION

* Consider the pattern of your own thoughts. What is your reaction to Proverbs 23:7?

* How can you seek first the kingdom of God?

✳ How can you lay up treasures in heaven?

✳ In what way does worry reflect a lack of faith? What does it say about your view of God?

✳ What steps can you take to combat worry with faith in your own life?

☼ DAY 5

Luke 12:13–21: *Then one from the crowd said to Him, "Teacher, tell my brother to divide the inheritance with me." But He said to him, "Man, who made Me a judge or an arbitrator over you?" And He said to them, "Take heed and beware of covetousness, for one's life does not consist in the abundance of the things he possesses." Then He spoke a parable to them, saying: "The ground of a certain rich man yielded plentifully. And he thought within himself, saying, 'What shall I do, since I have no room to store my crops?' So he said, 'I will do this: I will pull down my barns and build greater, and there I will store all my* *crops and my goods. And I will say to my soul, "Soul, you have many goods laid up for many years; take your ease; eat, drink, and be merry."' But God said to him, 'Fool! This night your soul will be required of you; then whose will those things be which you have provided?' So is he who lays up treasure for himself, and is not rich toward God."*

The tendency to trust in the empty promises of wealth and possessions is not a new ailment. People have always attempted to find value and meaning by acquiring things and accumulating wealth. How incredible that over the centuries we have not learned how pointless it is to trust in anything this world has to offer. It's like an endless cycle—we are born, we work and acquire, we die and leave it to the next generation; then they follow in our footsteps (Ecclesiastes 2:18–21). No wonder God calls our hopeless quest for material security foolish.

It's not that money is bad or possessing things is evil. The problem is when money and things possess us. When materialism is our god there is no room for any other. As we learned earlier, we cannot serve God and mammon (wealth, riches, possessions).

Even the world calls the quest for its own treasures a "rat race." We run around frantically to find our treasure and then scamper just as frantically to keep it. We behave much like rats in a maze—mindlessly pursuing our slice of cheese. But eventually the cheese is gone and we are hungry again.

In John 6:35, Jesus says, "I am the bread of life. He who comes to Me shall never hunger, and he who believes in Me shall never thirst." It is only through Him that we will be satisfied. It is only through Him that we find a fulfillment that will never come to an end.

QUESTIONS FOR REFLECTION

✳ How can you be "rich toward God"?

✳ Do you believe there is anything wrong with planning for tomorrow? Why or why not?

✳ What is your reaction to God calling the barn builder in Jesus' parable a "fool"? In what way can you relate to the actions of the foolish barn builder?

✳ What attitude is at the heart of the statement, "And I will say to my soul, 'Soul, you have many goods laid up for many years; take your ease; eat, drink, and be merry'"?

✳ Starting today, how can you begin to find your satisfaction in Jesus instead of in material wealth?

DEATH OF A DREAM

GROUP DISCUSSION

GETTING STARTED

Watch DVD session 5.

AFTER THE VIDEO

God cares more about who you're becoming than where you're going. You may recognize the wisdom in these words. But how do they look as a lifestyle—How do they affect the way you live?

God called Abram (Abraham) to leave behind everything familiar, to willingly lose everything that added security and comfort to his life, and to lay down all his own dreams. God called seventy-five-year-old Abram to go to an unknown place and begin again. God made Abram the man he was designed to be by placing new dreams in his heart.

Abram chose to follow where God's dream for him would lead. Along the way, it seemed even those dreams would die.

But in God's kingdom, death is not the end; it is the beginning. Through his willingness to let go of his dreams, Abram was able to experience his new life in God. Abram's dreams may have been good; God's dreams for him were amazing. Abram gave up everyday dreams for the extraordinary adventure of following God. Rather than spend his life in pursuit of a dream, Abram chose to give all his worship and attention to the only deserving One—his God and Father.

We all have dreams, and most of us dream of the same type of "perfect" future as the lure of the world vies for our full adoration. Our dreams for our own lives can even become idols that direct our every move. But God has better dreams waiting for us. He will make us the people He created us to be by placing specially chosen dreams within each individual heart. He has a plan for every life, and the dreams He places in each heart will accomplish His will in each life.

> Our dreams, no matter how great or noble they may be, will always make a lousy god.

In order for God to lead you into your own extraordinary adventure with Him, you must be willing to let your dreams die so God's dreams for you can live.

QUESTIONS FOR DISCUSSION

1. What is your most cherished dream?

2. "God cares more about who you're becoming than where you're going." Share your thoughts about this statement. Is this a new concept for you? How might this truth affect your life? Your faith?

3. What things in your life give you a sense of security and comfort? Do you have dreams connected to a certain "ideal" way of life? What are they?

4. If God called you to lay down your dreams to follow Him, what would be your reaction? Which dream or comfort would you find it hardest to leave behind?

5. Do you have a secret, deep-seated dream? What do you believe is the source of that dream?

6. If God calls you to face an unknown future in order to follow Him, what would be the most challenging aspect of that calling? What would cause you the most fear?

7. Read Jeremiah 29:11. What is your reaction to this verse?

PRAYER

Father, I praise you for creating me with a purpose. I thank you for the destiny you have planned for me. Help me to let go of my own dreams and embrace your dreams for me. I want to be all you created me to be and live out your will for my life. Help me to always find my peace and security within the shelter of your incredible love for me. May you always be my only Guide and the Source of all my comfort. In the name of your Son, my Savior Jesus Christ. Amen.

DAY BY DAY

When we read the stories of biblical characters who lived so long ago, it can be hard to realize they were people just like us. But like us, dreams lived in their hearts and, like us, they suffered disappointment and heartbreak when their dreams failed to be realized. This week, we are going to take a look at a dreamer who lived a life filled with suffering but who did not complain. He embraced God's dream for his life and enjoyed the blessings of a life totally in the center of God's will. Introducing . . . Joseph, son of Israel and dreamer of better things.

☀ DAY 1

Genesis 37:3–11: *Now Israel loved Joseph more than all his children, because he was the son of his old age. Also he made him a tunic of many colors. But when his brothers saw that their father loved him more than all his brothers, they hated him and could not speak peaceably to him. Now Joseph had a dream, and he told it to his brothers; and they hated him even more. So he said to them, "Please hear this dream which I have dreamed: There we were, binding sheaves in the field. Then behold, my sheaf arose and also stood upright; and indeed your sheaves stood all around and bowed down to my sheaf." And his brothers said to him, "Shall you indeed reign over us? Or shall you indeed have dominion over us?" So they hated him even more for his dreams and for his words. Then he dreamed still another dream and told it to his brothers, and said, "Look, I have dreamed another dream. And this time, the sun, the moon, and the eleven stars bowed down to me." So he told it to his father and his brothers; and his father rebuked him and said to him, "What is this dream that you have dreamed? Shall your mother and I and your brothers indeed come to bow down to the earth before you?" And his brothers envied him, but his father kept the matter in mind.*

Although Scripture doesn't tell us what young Joseph's hopes and dreams were for his future, we can only imagine he expected life to continue to be good. His father, Jacob (whose name God had changed to Israel), was a wealthy man with large herds of animals and many wives. Joseph most likely expected to follow in his father's footsteps. As one of Jacob's youngest sons, it was unlikely that he would inherit his father's wealth, but Joseph most likely dreamed of a future filled with all the good things life could bring.

God had a plan for Joseph beyond anything the young man could possibly imagine. He gave Joseph an amazing dream. Assuming Joseph was much like us, he most likely tried to fit the message of the dream into life as he knew it. He may well have thought the dream meant he would somehow end up inheriting all God had given his father. But the dreams Joseph held in his heart were about to die and be replaced by God's perfect plan for his life.

Joseph was so excited and optimistic about the dreams God gave him that he told his brothers. They didn't join him in his joy; it's not hard to imagine they felt threatened and insulted. After all, Joseph was obviously their father's favorite. What if Jacob decided to leave all his wealth to this little brother? Who did this kid think he was? How dare he try to raise himself above them?

When God places a dream in your heart, it's important that you allow Him to work it out. When you take matters into your own hands, you just might find yourself thrown into a pit of despair, just as Joseph did. You must be willing to leave your future in God's hands even as you embrace His perfect dream for your life.

QUESTIONS FOR REFLECTION

✳ What dreams do you have for your own future?

✳ Are these dreams your own or are they the dreams God has placed in your heart? How do you know?

✳ Have you ever experienced the death of a dream? In what ways can you see God's hand at work in the situation?

✳ In what way are your own dreams actually empty promises for the future?

✳ Read Jeremiah 29:11. How can this verse sustain you when your dreams die?

☀ DAY 2

Genesis 37:23–28: *So it came to pass, when Joseph had come to his brothers, that they stripped Joseph of his tunic, the tunic of many colors that was on him. Then they took him and cast him into a pit. And the pit was empty; there was no water in it. And they sat down to eat a meal. Then they lifted their eyes and looked, and there was a company of Ishmaelites, coming from Gilead with their camels, bearing spices, balm, and myrrh, on their way to carry them down to Egypt. So Judah said to his brothers, "What profit is there if we kill our brother and conceal his blood? Come and let us sell him to the Ishmaelites, and let not our hand be upon him, for he is our brother and our flesh." And his brothers listened. Then Midianite traders passed* *by; so the brothers pulled Joseph up and lifted him out of the pit, and sold him to the Ishmaelites for twenty shekels of silver. And they took Joseph to Egypt.*

Can you imagine the hurt Joseph must have felt when his brothers turned on him? The despair must have been overwhelming. One day he was clothed in a symbol of his father's love and was waiting for God to lift him up to the heights of honor; and the next, he was sitting in the bottom of a pit, cold, rejected, and alone. He must have felt heartbroken and hopeless as he watched his cherished dream seem to die before his tear-filled eyes.

We have already considered that God is the God of today—yesterday is gone, and tomorrow cannot be known by our limited, human minds. When God places a dream in our hearts, we can be tempted to define it for ourselves and set our own course for its fulfillment. But we cannot know what tomorrow holds, so any attempt to make our own dreams come true is useless. We end up chasing an empty promise instead of following God's plan for our lives.

Joseph couldn't have known as he sat in a deep, dark hole that God's plan for him had been set in motion. Before God could move Joseph forward into the future, Joseph's version of the dream had to die. Joseph had to come to a place where he did not trust in himself or what the world had to offer. He had to let go of his own dream and allow God to lead him to the destiny He intended.

QUESTIONS FOR REFLECTION

✳ In what ways have you attempted to make your dreams come true? What have been the results?

✳ How do you think you can tell the difference between your own dreams and the dreams God has given you?

✳ In what ways have you applied your own interpretations to the dreams God placed in your heart?

✳ With the story of Joseph in mind, consider your own life thus far. How have you found yourself in a "pit" as you have attempted to make your dreams a reality?

✳ In looking back at your life, can you see any time when God took you through a struggle in order to bring death to your own dreams and replace them with His will for your life? How did that change the course of your life?

☀ DAY **3**

Genesis 39:1–4: *Now Joseph had been taken down to Egypt. And Potiphar, an officer of Pharaoh, captain of the guard, an Egyptian, bought him from the Ishmaelites who had taken him down there. The Lord was with Joseph, and he was a successful man; and he was in the house of his master the Egyptian. And his master saw that the Lord was with him and that the Lord made all he did to prosper in his hand. So Joseph found favor in his sight, and served him. Then he made him overseer of his house, and all that he had he put under his authority.*

Genesis 39:11, 12: *But it happened about this time, when Joseph went into the house to do his work, and none of the men* *of the house was inside, that [Potiphar's wife] caught him by his garment, saying, "Lie with me." But he left his garment in her hand, and fled and ran outside.*

Genesis 39:19, 20: *So it was, when [Joseph's] master heard the words which [Potiphar's] wife spoke to him, saying, "Your servant did to me after this manner," that [Potiphar's] anger was aroused. Then Joseph's master took him and put him into the prison, a place where the king's prisoners were confined. And he was there in the prison.*

Genesis 39:22, 23: *And the keeper of the prison committed to Joseph's hand all the prisoners who were in the prison; whatever they did there, it was his doing. The keeper of the prison did not look into anything that was under Joseph's authority, because the Lord was with him; and whatever he did, the Lord made it prosper.*

If Joseph had felt despair in the pit, just imagine how he felt when he was falsely accused of attempted rape and thrown in prison. No doubt, his concept of a dream come true did not include trumped-up charges, a ruined reputation, and the total loss of freedom.

But Joseph did not allow circumstances to cause him to doubt God. Rather than consider his life over and his God-given dreams lost, Joseph accepted his fate and made the best of it. Even though he must have been quite confused by the seemingly out-of-control events, he trusted that God was most definitely in control.

As you walk through life, there will be many times when it will seem your life is running out of control. During those times, it's important to remember that the control should not be yours—it belongs to God. When you trust God to handle all your todays, your tomorrows will never be cause for fear and despair. God is the God of hope. When you let go of your own dreams in favor of His plan for your life, you can trust Him to lead you no matter what your eyes see or your mind perceives. God has a special dream crafted just for you to give you "a future and a hope" (Jeremiah 29:11).

QUESTIONS FOR REFLECTION

* Do you find it hard to trust God when your life seems to be falling apart? Why do you believe this is so?

* How different would your life look if you followed Joseph's example and saw even the worst circumstance as an opportunity for God to continue to act to bring about His plan?

✳ It's only reasonable to think Joseph suffered from the same emotional storms we would feel in his situation. What do his responses to bad situations tell us about whether we should allow feelings to determine our actions when dreams seem to die?

☀ DAY **4**

Genesis 41:1a: *Then it came to pass, at the end of two full years, that Pharaoh had a dream.*

Genesis 41:15, 16: *And Pharaoh said to Joseph, "I have had a dream, and there is no one who can interpret it. But I have heard it said of you that you can understand a dream, to interpret it." So Joseph answered Pharaoh, saying, "It is not in me; God will give Pharaoh an answer of peace."*

Genesis 41:25–36: *Then Joseph said to Pharaoh, "The dreams of Pharaoh are one; God has shown Pharaoh what He is about to do: The seven good cows are seven years, and the seven good heads are seven years; the dreams are one. And the seven thin and ugly cows which came up after them are seven years, and the seven empty heads blighted by the east wind are seven years of famine. This is the thing which I have spoken to Pharaoh. God has shown Pharaoh what He is about to do. Indeed seven years of great plenty will come throughout all the land of Egypt; but after them seven years of famine will arise, and all* *the plenty will be forgotten in the land of Egypt; and the famine will deplete the land. So the plenty will not be known in the land because of the famine following, for it will be very severe. And the dream was repeated to Pharaoh twice because the thing is established by God, and God will shortly bring it to pass. Now therefore, let Pharaoh select a discerning and wise man, and set him over the land of Egypt. Let Pharaoh do this, and let him appoint officers over the land, to collect one-fifth of the produce of the land of Egypt in the seven plentiful years. And let them gather all the food of those good years that are coming, and store up grain under the authority of Pharaoh, and let them keep food in the cities. Then that food shall be as a reserve for the land for the seven years of famine which shall be in the land of Egypt, that the land may not perish during the famine."*

Genesis 41:39–41: *Then Pharaoh said to Joseph, "Inasmuch as God has shown you all this, there is no one as discerning and wise as you. You shall be over my house, and all my people shall be ruled according to your word; only in regard to the throne will I be greater than you." And Pharaoh said to Joseph, "See, I have set you over all the land of Egypt."*

Joseph was a little brother turned dreamer, turned captive, turned slave, turned prisoner, turned interpreter, turned ruler. There is no way anyone could have anticipated the path God planned for Joseph. And certainly, no one would have imagined that the Israelite boy would one day rule Egypt.

Such are God's dreams for us. We can conjure up all kinds of dreams: wealth, power, fame; but all our best attempts at envisioning our future will pale in light of our God-dreamed destiny. Obviously, we aren't all meant to become rulers, but we all have a perfect destiny conceived in the mind of our heavenly Father. By taking us along a path of learning and discovery, as He did with Joseph, He will place within us all we need to fulfill His plan for our lives. We only need to let go of the empty promise of our own dreams and embrace God's dream for us. Then, like Joseph, we can change our world by living out God's perfect plan for our lives.

The path of Joseph's life was difficult, and he probably wondered if he had misunderstood God. But Joseph trusted God enough to be at peace no matter what his situation. He lived out Paul's words in Philippians 4:11, "I have learned in whatever state I am, to be content."

QUESTIONS FOR REFLECTION

✳ What are the dreams in your life that offer only empty promises?

✳ What dreams do you have that you believe to be God-given?

* Are you willing to trust God to lead you to the realization of His dreams for you no matter the difficulties you may face along the way?

* What do you believe will lead you to find contentment in every situation you face?

☼ DAY 5

Genesis 42:6–8: *Now Joseph was governor over the land; and it was he who sold to all the people of the land. And Joseph's brothers came and bowed down before him with their faces to the earth. Joseph saw his brothers and recognized them, but he acted as a stranger to them and spoke roughly to them. Then he said to them, "Where do you come from?" And they said, "From the land of Canaan to buy food." So Joseph recognized his brothers, but they did not recognize him.*

Genesis 43:24–28: *So the man brought the men into Joseph's house and gave them water, and they washed their feet; and he gave their donkeys feed. Then they made the present ready for Joseph's coming at noon, for they heard that they would eat bread there. And when Joseph came home, they brought him the*

present which was in their hand into the house, and bowed down
before him to the earth. Then he asked them about their well-
being, and said, "Is your father well, the old man of whom you
spoke? Is he still alive?" And they answered, "Your servant our
father is in good health; he is still alive." And they bowed their
heads down and prostrated themselves.

Genesis 45:1–8: *Then Joseph could not restrain himself be-*
fore all those who stood by him, and he cried out, "Make every-
one go out from me!" So no one stood with him while Joseph
made himself known to his brothers. And he wept aloud, and the
Egyptians and the house of Pharaoh heard it. Then Joseph said
to his brothers, "I am Joseph; does my father still live?" But his
brothers could not answer him, for they were dismayed in his
presence. And Joseph said to his brothers, "Please come near to
me." So they came near. Then he said: "I am Joseph your brother,
whom you sold into Egypt. But now, do not therefore be grieved
or angry with yourselves because you sold me here; for God sent
me before you to preserve life. For these two years the famine
has been in the land, and there are still five years in which there
will be neither plowing nor harvesting. And God sent me before
you to preserve a posterity for you in the earth, and to save your
lives by a great deliverance. So now it was not you who sent me
here, but God; and He has made me a father to Pharaoh, and lord
of all his house, and a ruler throughout all the land of Egypt.

God brought Joseph into the realization of the dream
placed in his heart as a very young man. By taking him along
a very difficult path, God had stripped Joseph's heart of his

limited and self-made dreams. He replaced the empty promises of Joseph's immature dreams with a promise of deliverance and a future filled with hope. All that Joseph seemed to have lost was returned to him. He had let go of his own dreams, allowed the death of his understanding of God's dream for him, and reaped the inevitable blessing that trusting God will always bring.

So much about Joseph's journey can teach us about how to handle the death of a dream and hold to the certain hope that comes from trusting God and His plan for our lives. God will never let us down. He knows our future and wants to fill us with the peace and contentment our hearts desire. By following Joseph's example, we can rest in the knowledge that God has a perfect plan for our lives no matter where our journey may take us.

Joseph began his life with a dream. His journey took him through times of want and confusion. He seemed to lose everything he treasured. But in the end, the dream he was given when very young was brought to reality in the most unexpected, miraculous way. The man who was once a slave ended up serving and ruling with the king. Such is our eternal destiny when we trust God and obediently follow His path for our lives. Revelation 20:6 says of those who love and serve the Lord, "They shall be priests of God and of Christ, and shall reign with Him a thousand years." We will rule and reign with our King!

QUESTIONS FOR REFLECTION

✳ How might Joseph's immature dreams have become an idol in his life?

✳ What part did humility play in Joseph's realization of his God-given dream?

✳ How might the insight you've gained from Joseph's life enable you to more effectively face difficulties in the future?

✳ Do you find it difficult to trust God when it seems your life is falling apart? Why or why not?

✳ How can the empty promises of our self-made dreams rob us of God's best for our lives?

✳ In light of Joseph's journey, what heart attitudes will enable you to watch your God-given dreams become reality?

SOUL SATISFACTION

GROUP DISCUSSION

GETTING STARTED

Watch DVD session 6.

AFTER THE VIDEO

It's not just the Rolling Stones who can't get no satisfaction. The entire world screams it out in actions and words. We run around in frantic hope of finding the "thing" that will cure the emptiness and fill our hope-starved lives with purpose and destiny. Who are we? What are we? Why are we here? These questions drive us to find answers. But we will never find what we seek in the world around us; we can never discover our ultimate destiny in the created because we can only find our true identity through the Creator.

As a mirror reflects the truth of what it sees, so we are to reflect the image of God. This is who we are, what we are, and why we're here. If we attempt to answer life's questions by reflecting the idols we've built or the dreams we've manu-factured, we deny our true purpose. Self-constructed answers will never fill us; idols will never provide the joy and peace of fulfillment. Not only will they leave us empty and wanting, they will rob us of our ability to find true satisfaction. Total soul satisfaction of purpose and meaning can only be found in God.

We find our purpose, our destiny,
in the One who created us.

QUESTIONS FOR DISCUSSION

1. What do you see when you look in the mirror?

2. Have you found true satisfaction in your own life? If not, why? If yes, how?

3. Do you think everyone struggles with the questions of who we are, what we are, and why we're here? Why do you believe that is so?

4. Why do you think we attempt to find the answers to those questions in the world around us?

5. Where should we find those answers? Why? How?

6. What are the self-constructed answers you've turned to for fulfillment?

7. What idols have left you wanting more?

8. What is your definition of "total soul satisfaction"? How do you believe you can find it and maintain it?

9. How has our study of empty promises and the discovery of soul satisfaction impacted your life? What are the greatest truths you've discovered? What does tomorrow look like for you in light of these discoveries?

PRAYER

Father, we thank you that fulfillment and true soul satisfaction can be found in you and your plan for our lives. We want to live out the destiny you planned for us. We want your dream for us to become our dream. Help us to recognize the idols in our lives and learn to serve you. We ask you to help us deny the lure of empty promises and teach us to grab hold of all you have for us. It is our desire to serve you and live in the peace and contentment only you can provide. In Jesus' precious name we pray. Amen.

DAY BY DAY

Nothing can destroy our chance of soul satisfaction as much as getting caught in the vicious cycle of relying on empty promises. It's a useless attempt to discover purpose and meaning by our own efforts. All we do is wear ourselves out. In the end, all we will have to show for our efforts is a trail of broken dreams littered with discontent. Our useless attempts to find satisfaction will end up stealing the promise of our future: by refusing to rely on God to lead us to our destiny, our dreams will die a final death; by following the empty promises of the idols in our lives, our hopes will be destroyed.

John 10:10 says, "The thief does not come except to steal, and to kill, and to destroy." We have an enemy who fills our minds with empty promises. He tries to make us believe his lies and cling to them rather than God. We must realize our true enemy is not the temptation to believe and chase empty promises; our enemy is the one through whom the temptation comes—Satan. He's the one trying to mess us up and sell us a bill of goods.

DAY 1

Genesis 1:27: *So God created man in His own image; in the image of God He created him; male and female He created them.*

Proverbs 3:6: *In all your ways acknowledge Him, and He shall direct your paths.*

We are made in the image of God. Most of us are very familiar with that truth, but do we really grasp all that it means? It's not about how we look; it's about who we are. We are the children of almighty God—the King of Creation. We are citizens of His kingdom. We have been given the very image of our Father and King. He gave us His own image so the world can see its rightful Ruler. We should reflect to the world the One who created us and the One we serve.

When we realize who we are and whose image we bear, we learn our true identity. We acknowledge God's rightful place as our Ruler and King, and our souls find contentment and security in Him. Real and pure soul satisfaction fills our hearts and minds, and we discover true purpose and meaning. When we recognize that God is the only One who can fill the emptiness within us, we are completed and our entire selves respond with gratitude and thanksgiving—a heart of worship toward God is born.

In worshipping God, we will find ourselves becoming more fully like Him, reflecting in our lives the character of the One we worship. Once we know and recognize God's right to rule our lives, the empty promises of this world no longer have the same power to deceive us. We are freed to follow Him into the destiny He has prepared for us.

QUESTIONS FOR REFLECTION

✳ How does knowing you are made in the image of God affect the way you see yourself? Your world?

✳ How do we acknowledge Him in all our ways?

✳ How might acknowledging Him in all our ways enable us to more effectively follow where he leads?

✳ How can a person whose heart is filled with worship for God be less likely to fall for the empty promises of this world?

✳ What does "worship" mean to you?

✳ How might your entire life be an act of worship toward God?

 DAY **2**

Ephesians 6:10–13: *Finally, my brethren, be strong in the Lord and in the power of His might. Put on the whole armor of God, that you may be able to stand against the wiles of the devil. For we do not wrestle against flesh and blood, but against principalities, against powers, against the rulers of the darkness of this age, against spiritual hosts of wickedness in the heavenly places. Therefore take up the whole armor of God, that you may be able to withstand in the evil day, and having done all, to stand.*

1 Peter 5:8: *Be sober, be vigilant; because your adversary the devil walks about like a roaring lion, seeking whom he may devour.*

Even those who realize their true identity as citizens of God's kingdom and have found soul satisfaction in knowing and serving Him can be led astray by empty promises. People are simply imperfect, and our relationship with God will never be perfected in this life. The temptation to trust in empty promises will always haunt us on this side of eternity.

Though it may be inevitable that we will not perfectly follow God's plan for us, it is still amazing how empty promises can beckon us and tempt us away from our God-given destiny. Why is it that after we see person after person *not* being satisfied by empty promises we think it will be somehow different for us? Why are we so convinced that what happens to others could never happen on our unique journey? Do we honestly think things will be different in our case? Are we really that dumb? Or do we have someone speaking things to us? Lying to us? And, what's worse, making us think it's not him speaking?

Satan has been fooling humanity in just that way since the beginning of time. He plants thoughts in our minds and then stands back and watches as we believe his lies instead of the Word of God. The Bible tells us, "Delight yourself also in the LORD, and He shall give you the desires of your heart" (Psalm 37:4). Yet we turn to the empty promises of worldly delights and expect our desires to be fulfilled.

If we realize we are victims of a vicious attack, we can effectively fight our enemy and win. We can find protection from Satan's mental assault by standing strong on the truth of God's Word and turning our backs on our enemy's schemes.

QUESTIONS FOR REFLECTION

✳ What are the idols that tempt you?

Session 6

✳ What does it mean to live a sober and vigilant life?

✳ How can you "take up the whole armor of God"?

✳ What are the desires of your heart? What are the empty promises Satan tries to make you believe?

☼ DAY 3

Ephesians 6:14–17: *Stand therefore, having girded your waist with truth, having put on the breastplate of righteousness, and having shod your feet with the preparation of the gospel of peace; above all, taking the shield of faith with which you will be able to quench all the fiery darts of the wicked one. And take the helmet of salvation, and the sword of the Spirit, which is the word of God.*

James 4:7: *Therefore submit to God. Resist the devil and he will flee from you.*

There is no doubt that we have a powerful enemy. Satan has been around since before man was created. He was there when God formed Adam. He knows how and why we were created, so he knows exactly how to tempt us away from God's plan for us. You see, Satan hates us simply because God loves us. In his desire to be equal with God, Satan turned from God and is trying to get man to do the same thing.

Satan knows of our need to find meaning and purpose. He knows God created each of us to know Him and walk with Him into a unique destiny. He realizes the all-consuming nature of our desire to discover who we are and why we're here. And he uses his knowledge against us. He tries to fill our lives with counterfeit gods to keep us from knowing and serving our Creator—almighty God, who loves us and wants to fill our hearts and lives with Himself.

Satan also knows he has no power over us except deception. But when we understand and accept that true soul satisfaction can be ours only through knowing and serving God, it becomes easier to stand against Satan's lies. He is very aware that his ability to deceive those who know, believe, and live out God's Word is seriously lessened. It's not that those who serve the Lord are immune to the enemy's tactics; we are simply prepared to resist them. If we stand strong in the truth of God's Word and meet the enemy's attacks with a sure faith in the Lord's power, we can break the vicious cycle of empty promises. We can be victorious over our enemy whenever we submit to God's plan for our lives.

QUESTIONS FOR REFLECTION

✳ Is the concept that our attempt to find soul satisfaction through empty promises is a scheme of our enemy a new one for you?

✳ How might this realization change the way you respond to the attraction of false gods in your life?

✳ How might this realization help you detect Satan's lies more easily?

✳ What steps can you take to prepare yourself to "submit to God" and "resist the devil"?

DAY **4**

Matthew 4:1–11: *Then Jesus was led up by the Spirit into the wilderness to be tempted by the devil. And when He had fasted forty days and forty nights, afterward He was hungry. Now when the tempter came to Him, he said, "If You are the Son of God, command that these stones become bread." But He answered and said, "It is written, 'Man shall not live by bread alone, but by every word that proceeds from the mouth of God.'" Then the devil took Him up into the holy city, set Him on the pinnacle of the temple, and said to Him, "If You are the Son of God, throw Yourself down. For it is written: 'He shall give His angels charge over you,' and, 'In their hands they shall bear you up, lest you dash your foot against a stone.'" Jesus said to him, "It is written again, 'You shall not tempt the Lord your God.'" Again, the devil took Him up on an exceedingly high mountain, and showed Him all the kingdoms of the world and their glory. And he said to Him, "All these things I will give You if You will fall down and worship me." Then Jesus said to him, "Away with you, Satan! For it is written, 'You shall worship the Lord your God, and Him only you shall serve.'" Then the devil left Him, and behold, angels came and ministered to Him.*

Satan tempted Jesus by holding out to Him the things He wanted and needed most. Jesus was starving after a forty-day fast, so Satan tried to get Him to turn away from God's plan in order to fill his hunger. Jesus was extremely weary from days in the wilderness, so Satan tempted Him to have angels come to His aid. Jesus is fully God, but He had left heaven and become fully human, so Satan tempted Him by offering Him the power and authority it seemed the Son of God should rightfully expect.

The way Satan tempts us is very similar. He says to our needy, unfulfilled souls, "I will give you . . ." Satan promises money, sex, power, or whatever else we think will make us happy. Look at the way he tempted Eve—by making her believe there was something she needed that God had not given her. Consider how he used Judas—by offering him what he prized the most: money.

You may look at the account of Satan's temptation of Jesus and think, "But He was God's Son. I can't be as strong as He was." Well, Jesus said, "You shall receive power when the Holy Spirit has come upon you" (Acts 1:8). He also said, "Most assuredly, I say to you, he who believes in Me, the works that I do he will do also; and greater works than these he will do, because I go to My Father" (John 4:12). Jesus sent you the Holy Spirit to enable you to stand strong in this world and successfully fight the enemy, just as He did.

Even after you have been walking with the Lord a long time and trying to live in the power of the Holy Spirit, you may never completely escape the lure of empty promises and idolatry. But hopefully, as you mature, you will become even more aware that this battle against Satan will continue. This is a lifelong war, and you need to be prepared to fight it.

QUESTIONS FOR REFLECTION

✳ What are the things Satan uses to tempt you to turn away from God and follow his empty promises?

✳ How have you fought these temptations in the past? Have you been successful? Why do you believe this is so?

✳ How can the awareness that your fight against Satan's schemes is lifelong help prepare you to win each individual battle?

✳ In what ways have you experienced the power of the Holy Spirit in your life thus far?

Session 6

✳ How do you now view the role of the Holy Spirit in your quest to deny the idols in your life and follow faithfully where God leads?

☀ DAY **5**

1 Corinthians 13:12: *For now we see in a mirror, dimly, but then face to face. Now I know in part, but then I shall know just as I also am known.*

1 John 3:2: *Beloved, now we are children of God; and it has not yet been revealed what we shall be, but we know that when He is revealed, we shall be like Him, for we shall see Him as He is.*

Revelation 21:3–7: *And I heard a loud voice from heaven saying, "Behold, the tabernacle of God is with men, and He will dwell with them, and they shall be His people. God Himself will be with them and be their God. And God will wipe away every tear from their eyes; there shall be no more death, nor sorrow, nor crying. There shall be no more pain, for the former things have passed away." Then He who sat on the throne said, "Behold, I make all things new." And He said to me, "Write, for these words are true and faithful." And He said to me, "It is done! I am the Alpha and the Omega, the Beginning and the End. I will give of the fountain of the water of life freely to him who thirsts. He who overcomes shall inherit all things, and I will be his God and he shall be My son."*

In this life, no matter how hard we seek God and God alone, there will still be a tinge of emptiness springing forth from within our soul. Though diligently seeking God certainly brings purpose, satisfaction, and value to life, we will still feel somehow incomplete.

Why?

We can't be totally satisfied and content, because we're not home. We think what we want is a bigger title, better looks, more popularity, larger sums of money, the perfect spouse. However, what we really want is the person we were made for, Jesus, and the place we were made for, heaven. Until the day we go to be with God, we will be filled with an unnamed yearning to be in the place for which we were created, the physical presence of God.

No matter how hard we seek after God, the relationship we have with Him in this present world will never be as rich, fulfilling, or freeing as the one we will know in heaven. But this doesn't mean we should just give up.

We have a choice to make. We can either take our inner emptiness to God, trusting Him for our eventual fulfillment, or we can make the decision to fend for ourselves, turning to empty promises that will only further compound our inner emptiness. Each and every moment is an opportunity, a choice: we may either draw closer to the likeness and presence of our Creator by seeking Him with all we have and all we are, or we may choose to drift further away from Him and

His plan for our lives by believing our enemy's lies and falling for the empty promises of this world.

QUESTIONS FOR REFLECTION

✳ As you come to the end of this study, what new insight has most impacted your life?

✳ What do you think you will feel when you are taken into the presence of almighty God?

✳ What steps can you make that could enable you to more easily make a daily choice to draw closer to God?

✳ Revelation 21:7 says, "He who overcomes shall inherit all things, and I will be his God and he shall be My son." What is your reaction to this verse?

✳ How might keeping the promise of Revelation 21:7 always in mind help you to deny the lure of empty promises and focus on seeking God?

CONCLUSION

Until the day we see Jesus face to face, we will continue to feel the yearning within that can never truly be filled. We may not be aware of the source of our nagging emptiness, but until we look into those eyes and feel the touch of those nail-scarred hands, we will never know complete soul satisfaction.

We were created to love and serve the Lord. We were created to be in His presence. There will be void in our lives as long as we are separated from the One who created us.

Until the day arrives that we, like the thief on the cross, hear the words our souls long for—"This day, you shall be with me in Paradise"—we will continue to seek fulfillment. While we are still in this world, we can find relief from the longing by living our entire lives on an all-out search for God. First Chronicles 28:9 contains a promise. Read this verse and watch for it: "Know the God of your father, and serve Him with a loyal heart and with a willing mind; for the LORD searches all hearts and understands all the intent of the thoughts. If you seek Him, He will be found by you." Deuteronomy 4:29 says, "You will seek the LORD your God, and you will find Him if you seek Him with all your heart and with all your soul." These verses offer the same promise: seek God with all you are, and you will find Him. We can cling to that promise as we reach out with empty hearts and hands to the only One who can fill them.

"Today, if you will hear His voice, do not harden your hearts" (Hebrews 4:7). Listen to the voice of God as He invites you to give up your idols and simply worship Him. Our Father alone is worthy of your whole devotion.

He, alone, has the authority to forgive your sins.

He, alone, has the wisdom to guide your whole life.

He, alone, has the power to fill the gnawing emptiness you feel.

He, alone, is God. Your soul doesn't crave something from Him; it craves Him.

> **Ephesians 1:15–23**: *Therefore I also, after I heard of your faith in the Lord Jesus and your love for all the saints, do not cease to give thanks for you, making mention of you in my prayers: that the God of our Lord Jesus Christ, the Father of glory, may give to you the spirit of wisdom and revelation in the knowledge of Him, the eyes of your understanding being enlightened; that you may know what is the hope of His calling, what are the riches of the glory of His inheritance in the saints, and what is the exceeding greatness of His power toward us who believe, according to the working of His mighty power which He worked in Christ when He raised Him from the dead and seated Him at His right hand in the heavenly places, far above all principality and power and might and dominion, and every name that is named, not only in this age but also in that which is to come. And He put all things under His feet, and gave Him to be head over all things to the church, which is His body, the fullness of Him who fills all in all.*

Matthew 11:29: *Take My yoke upon you and learn from Me, for I am gentle and lowly in heart, and you will find rest for your souls.*